D0266274

Great Journeys Across Earth

HILLARY AND NORGAY'S MOUNT EVEREST ADVENTURE

Jim Kerr

Heinemann
LIBRARY

www.heinemann.co.uk/library

Visit our website to find out more information about Heinemann Library books.

To order:

☎ Phone 44 (0) 1865 888066

▤ Send a fax to 44 (0) 1865 314091

▯ Visit the Heinemann Bookshop at www.heinemann.co.uk/library to browse our catalogue and order online.

Produced for Heinemann Library by
Monkey Puzzle Media Ltd
Gissing's Farm, Fressingfield,
Suffolk IP21 5SH, UK

First published in Great Britain by
Heinemann Library, Halley Court, Jordan Hill,
Oxford, OX2 8EJ, part of Harcourt Education.
Heinemann is a registered trademark of
Harcourt Education Ltd.

Editorial: Steve Parker and Louise Galpine
Design: Patrick Nugent and Victoria Bevan
Picture Research: Lynda Lines
Production: Severine Ribierre
Originated by Modern Age
Printed and bound in Hong Kong
13 digit ISBN 978 0 431 19125 6
12 11 10 09 08
10 9 8 7 6 5 4 3 2 1

British Library Cataloguing in Publication Data
Kerr, James
Hillary and Norgay's Mount Everest adventure.
- (Great journeys across Earth)
1. Hillary, Edmund, Sir - Juvenile literature 2.
Tenzing Norgay, 1914-1986 - Juvenile literature
3. Mount Everest Expedition (1953) - Juvenile
literature 4. Mountaineering expeditions - Everest,
Mount (China and Nepal) - History - Juvenile
literature 5. Everest, Mount (China and Nepal)
- Juvenile literature
 I. Title
 796.5'22'0922

Acknowledgements

Alamy pp. **5** (Worldwide Picture Library), **32–33**
(Oyvind Martinsen); Corbis pp. **28** (Bettmann),
40 (Reuters); Illustrated London News p. **7**;
Nature Picture Library pp. **16–17** (Leo and
Mandy Dickinson); NI Syndication p. **39**; Royal
Geographical Society pp. **4, 6, 9, 12, 13, 14, 15,
18–19, 19, 20, 21, 22, 23, 25, 27, 29, 31, 35, 36, 37**;
Science Photo Library p. **10** (A.C. Twomey); Still
Pictures pp. **24** (Tom Murphy/WWI), **41** (Oldrich
Karasek); Topfoto p. **38**. Artwork on page **26**
by Michael Posen. Maps by Martin Darlison at
Encompass Graphics.

Cover photograph of Mount Everest reproduced
with permission of Getty Images (Alan Kearney).

Title page photograph: Edmund Hillary and Tenzing
Norgay climb towards the summit of Mount Everest
in May 1953.

Expert Reader: Dr Paulette Posen, environmental
research scientist at the University of East Anglia

Every effort has been made to contact copyright
holders of any material reproduced in this book.
Any omissions will be rectified in subsequent
printings if notice is given to the publishers.

The paper used to print this book comes from
sustainable resources.

Disclaimer

All the Internet addresses (URLs) given in this book
were valid at the time of going to press. However,
due to the dynamic nature of the Internet, some
addresses may have changed or ceased to exist
since publication. While the author and publishers
regret any inconvenience this may cause readers,
no responsibility for any such changes can be
accepted by either the author or the publishers.

Contents

Some words are shown in bold, **like this**. You can find out what they mean by looking in the glossary.

On Top of the World

For 15 minutes, Edmund Hillary and Tenzing Norgay stood on top of the world. They were the first climbers to reach the top, or **summit**, of Mount Everest, the highest mountain on Earth. Looking down onto the snow, ice, and rock stretching thousands of metres below, they knew that they had climbed higher than anyone before.

Mission accomplished

It was late morning on Friday 29 May 1953 and the two men had been climbing since sunrise at 6:30 a.m. They had little time to take in the breathtaking views and think about what they had achieved. Both men were exhausted and the oxygen supplies that helped them to breathe were low. But they needed photographs to show the world that they had succeeded in their mission. Hillary took a picture of Norgay standing on the summit, his **ice axe** raised in victory, and then hurriedly photographed their route to the top.

Frostbite
*Hillary and Norgay were aware of the dangers of **frostbite**. This is damage to the skin and body parts, especially the fingers, toes, ears, and nose, caused by extreme cold. It is a danger high in the mountains. The Everest climbers wore three pairs of special gloves. There was only one case of frostbite on the journey.*

Tenzing Norgay stands on the summit of Mount Everest, raising the flags of Great Britain, Nepal, the United Nations, and India.

The summit of giant Mount Everest is the highest place on Earth.

Leaving their mark

Both climbers buried a few personal belongings in the snow. Hillary's was a small cross. Norgay, whose mother called Mount Everest "The Mountain So High No Bird Can Fly Over It", left some sweets and a present he had been given by his young daughter. The gifts were thanks to the spirits that had guided them safely to the top.

One final look

The two men rested for a few minutes and shared a piece of mint cake. Some sugary food for energy was just what they needed to help them on the long downwards climb, or descent. They had one final look at the snowy peaks and valleys stretching as far as their eyes could see. Then it was time to put on their heavy backpacks and leave.

Everest — the Ultimate Challenge

People known as **Sherpas** live in the Himalaya mountain range, where Everest is. They have worked as guides and porters for many expeditions, and the word "sherpa" has come to mean someone who carries loads. Sherpas call Everest *Sagarmatha*. This name may come from two Sherpa words. *Saga* means "sky" and *matha* means "forehead". For a Sherpa, to be on top of Mount Everest was to have your head in the clouds.

Himalayas

The Himalayas began to form about 50 million years ago. Deep below the land and sea lies Earth's crust, which is made of giant slabs or plates of rock. These plates move very slowly, about one centimetre (half an inch) per year. Two plates moving towards each other create a force which bends and pushes the rocks upwards. This is how the Himalayas were created.

Glaciers

*At the top of very high mountains, such as those in the Himalayas, deep snow lies on the ground all year round. This snow forms into layers of ice which flow very slowly down the mountain. This moving "river" of ice is a **glacier**.*

The Everest climbers crawled or walked over dangerous areas using ladders, or even log bridges, brought along specially for the purpose.

Mallory, fallen hero

By 1953 several expeditions had already failed to reach the top of Mount Everest. Before Hillary and Norgay, the most famous was in 1924. Two British climbers who took part, George Mallory and Sandy Irvine, disappeared near the top. Mallory's frozen body was discovered 75 years later. A medical examination showed that he had fallen badly. To this day, no one knows if the two climbers reached the **summit**.

Everest by numbers

- *The Himalayas are a range of mountains more than 2,500 kilometres (1,550 miles) from west to east.*
- *Everest is the tallest mountain, 8,850 metres (29,035 feet) high.*
- *Everest continues to grow by about one centimetre (about half an inch) per year.*
- *The temperature at the top of the mountain can be as low as -70°C (-94°F).*
- *More than 180 people have died trying to climb the mountain.*

The 1924 Everest expedition team included two climbers who died in the attempt. They are Irvine at the back left, and Mallory beside him.

Planning the expedition

In the summer of 1952, a three-way race was on to climb Mount Everest. An expedition team from Switzerland had failed to reach the top in May but planned to try again in the autumn. A French expedition was planning an attempt in the spring of 1953. The British were also desperate to be first to climb to the summit.

Mission control

Every part of the expedition had to be well planned. This began in a small office in London, UK. The expedition would be led by Eric Shipton, who believed that the journey should be made by a small team with basic supplies.

Shipton began to choose people for the journey, but there was a sudden change of plan. Previous attempts to climb Everest by small teams had failed. It was decided that this journey would use a big team with the latest equipment and plenty of supplies. A new leader, John Hunt, was appointed.

National rivalry

The contest to climb Everest first was mainly a matter of national pride. In the troubled years following the terrible Second World War (1939–1945), countries were eager to show their ability to organize events, be successful, and make good news around the world. Conquering Everest would boost a nation's self-esteem.

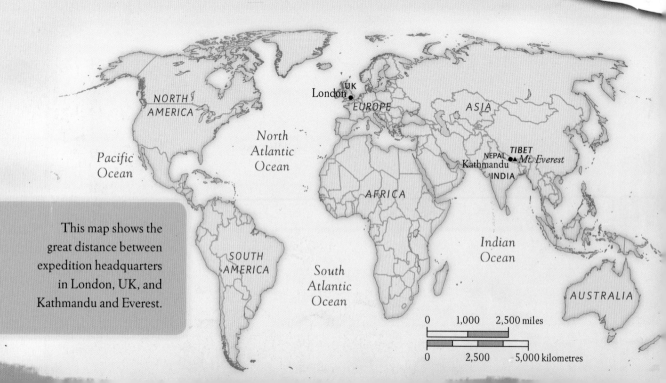

This map shows the great distance between expedition headquarters in London, UK, and Kathmandu and Everest.

Rush to start

The organizers could not afford to waste any more time. News came through that the second Swiss attempt had nearly succeeded, but the climbers had been forced back from very close to the summit. The Swiss team would surely try again a third time, and very soon.

Assembly

Planning continued in the autumn of 1952. Maps of Mount Everest were studied, and the very latest mountaineering equipment was tested. Food and other supplies were given by generous supporters to help the expedition. All of these supplies had to be shipped from London to India. The supplies would then be taken overland to the city of Kathmandu, the capital of Nepal. Then the expedition would begin. When the supply ship set sail from London on 12 February 1953, it carried more than 440 expedition packages.

Expedition supplies and equipment arrived by ship in India, and were then taken overland to Kathmandu for unpacking.

A Foothold on the Mountain

In March of 1953, the expedition team began to arrive in Kathmandu. The team got ready to make their way east, to the Himalayas and Mount Everest.

Grand send-off

Fourteen climbers and more than thirty **Sherpas** made up the expedition team. They met at the British **Embassy**, where a party was held to send them on their way. The gardens were littered with piles of supply boxes and packages to take on the journey. Many of the team members met each other for the first time on this day.

Yaks are part of the Sherpa way of life, especially for carrying goods. Here they wait in front of the Mount Everest **Base Camp**.

Yaks

*Yaks are animals found in the Himalayas. They are similar to cows, with long horns. Their long, shaggy hair helps them to keep warm. Yaks are kept for milk, meat, and skins, and for their hair which is used to make clothes and textiles. Sherpas use yaks to carry goods across mountain **passes**. They are also used to support climbing and trekking expeditions.*

March to the mountain

Nearly 400 people set off from Kathmandu on 10 March. More than 350 of these were local men and women who were hired to carry supplies to the site of the first camp. For 17 days, they walked through the Nepalese countryside. Many of the climbers describe this wonderful journey in their diaries and **journals**. It was spring in Nepal, and the weather was perfect. The sun shone and flowers, trees, birds, and other wildlife were everywhere.

On the march

John Hunt said of the Himalayan scenery along their marching route:

"...trees whose blossoms graduated from scarlet to pink, white, and yellow..."

Stronger and fitter

There was plenty of time for the team to relax along the way. They swam, read, and enjoyed the excellent meals made by the expedition cook. By marching about 15 kilometres (10 miles) each day, the explorers were also making themselves fitter and stronger for the adventure ahead.

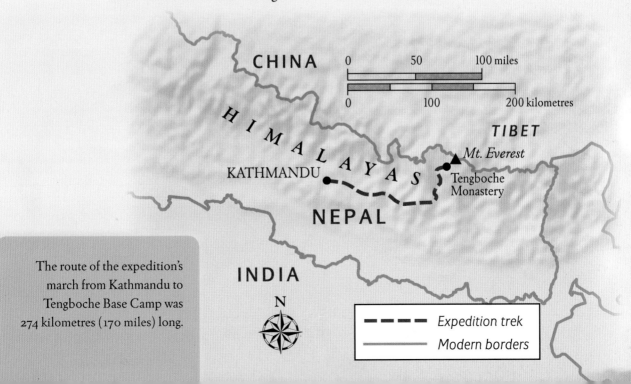

The route of the expedition's march from Kathmandu to Tengboche Base Camp was 274 kilometres (170 miles) long.

Base Camp

The Sherpas are people with strong spiritual beliefs. If the climbers did not know this already, they soon learned at Base Camp, the starting point for the climb. This was set up near the Tengboche (Thyangboche) **Monastery**.

A special place

The Sherpas follow a religion called **Buddhism** and the monastery was a very important centre for them. The Buddhist religion teaches its believers to practise kindness in all parts of their lives. The monks who lived at the monastery cooked simple meals for the visitors. They also prayed for the safety and success of the expedition.

Mountain boots

At Base Camp, the climbers replaced the shoes they had worn on the march with mountaineering boots. The team who would climb to the highest points on Everest wore boots that were specially made for each wearer. Although they were very large, the boots were light and warm.

First Base Camp was set up at Tengboche Monastery, after the 17-day overland trek from Kathmandu.

Setting up camp

Base Camp was set up and the team began to organize their climbing gear. They opened their boxes of supplies and sorted out which ones to carry up the mountain, to the various camps they would set up along the way. The team stayed at Base Camp for three weeks, planning their climbs. They practised with their climbing equipment on local cliffs and piles of rocks, and tried to get used to the thin air of the high mountains.

In this team photograph, leader John Hunt is sixth from the left in the back row, with Hillary and Norgay on either side.

Terminal moraines

*As a **glacier** slides slowly downwards, it scrapes off small pieces of rock and carries them along on its sides and base. At the end, or terminus, of the glacier, it is warmer and the ice melts. As this happens the rocks are left as piles called **terminal moraines**, which are a common feature in mountainous country.*

Ready to go

In early April 1953, Base Camp was moved from near Tengboche Monastery to a second main base, the Lake Camp, higher up by a lake on a glacier. John Hunt organized practice climbs and fitness training. The climbers had to get used to the conditions, especially the high **altitude** and problems such as ice-covered rocks and deep **crevasses**.

Edmund Hillary

*Edmund Hillary (born 1919) learned to climb at home in New Zealand. He worked with his father on a farm. Most of the family's money came from selling honey made by the bees they kept. When the honey-making season was over, Hillary went on mountaineering trips. This freedom to explore, together with his energy and determination, had made him one of the world's top **mountaineers**.*

Edmund Hillary, here at Camp IV, often wore his favourite blue striped headgear.

The problems of altitude

At the top of high mountains, the air is thinner and there is less oxygen available to breathe. Climbers high in the mountains become physically tired more quickly. Also, their ability to think clearly is affected.

To adjust to these conditions, climbers needs to **acclimatize**, or get used to, the lower oxygen levels. They must do this even if they have been to high altitudes before. In order to climb higher than 7,000 metres (23,000 feet), most climbers need equipment that allows them to breathe extra oxygen.

Tenzing Norgay

Tenzing Norgay (1914–1986), like many of the best Sherpa climbers, worked as a mountaineer. By 1953, he had already been on several Everest expeditions. He was larger than most Sherpas and very strong. Together with his experience, this made him a natural sirdar, or leader of Sherpas. He had been part of the Swiss expedition which almost succeeded in 1952. The Swiss climbers joked that Norgay had "three lungs". The imaginary extra one helped his breathing in the thin air high up the mountain.

Tenzing Norgay's mother Kinzom came to Tengboche Monastery, to check that he was fit and well before the climb!

Advance from Base Camp

The first big challenge for the leading climbers began on 13 April. Four men were selected by John Hunt for a difficult mission. Roped together for safety, they walked into the Khumbu **Icefall** at dawn.

Icefalls

When a **glacier** moves over a ridge in the land beneath, the ice cracks and breaks into huge blocks that slide down the steeper slopes. Climbers could fall into a deep **crevasse**, or be buried under a falling tower of ice, called a **serac**. John Hunt called the Khumbu Icefall "a monster". Looking up, the climbers saw house-sized blocks of cracked, creaking, unstable ice. Below them were the edges of deep crevasses. The mission of the climbers was to find a way through!

The tiny climbers near the bottom show the massive size of the Khumbu Icefall.

Snow blindness
The glare of the early morning sunshine on freshly laid snow is so bright, it can cause a form of blindness. The 1953 climbing team wore special snow goggles to prevent this problem.

On the Khumbu Icefall

The climbers needed to mark a safe route for the **Sherpas** who were to follow, bringing supplies. Flags were planted in the snow to mark the route. The climbers fixed ropes and ladders up steep ice cliffs. They tested and strengthened unstable **snow bridges**, which are layers of snow across a crevasse. They cut steps into the ice around dangerous ice towers.

The climbers managed to find a way into the middle of the Khumbu Icefall, where they were able to set up Camp II and take a short rest. Then they pushed on to the top of the icefall.

Climbing techniques

• *Climbers use ropes for safety. If one climber slips down a ledge or into a crevasse, the others can try to hold the rope tight and pull the climber up again.*

• ***Ice axes*** *are used to cut a series of steps into the steepest snow and ice slopes. Higher up the mountain, the steps needed to be huge for the climbers' high-**altitude** boots.*

Camp III

Camp III was set up at the top of the Khumbu Icefall. The expedition had reached a height of more than 6,100 metres (20,013 feet). At night, the temperature was well below freezing. Early morning sun glittered on the next part of their journey, a massive valley of snow called the Western **Cwm**. High in the sky above, the wind howled around the upper slopes of the mountain, whipping the snow off the top of Everest.

To be the best

The climbers were keen to prove their fitness, courage, and skill to leader John Hunt. He would select the very best individuals for the attempt to reach the top of the mountain, the final assault. They might impress him by volunteering for tricky missions. Or they could show great strength and stamina during exhausting days in the deep snowfields or when cutting **ice steps**.

Sherpas took loads of supplies between the camps, trekking day after day as part of the team.

Beware!

A team of 50 climbers, Sherpas, and carriers transported supplies through the icefall to Camp III. This was a difficult mission. Freshly fallen snow had buried many of the marker flags set up by the leading team. The carrying team had to watch every step, as the slowly moving icefall was constantly changing. Crevasses grew wider within a few days. One snow bridge was crossed safely by the lead climbers, but later it shattered after just a light tap with an ice axe!

It was time for the lead climbers to press on through the Western Cwm. They wanted to set up Camp IV above it, which would then become the expedition's Advance **Base Camp**.

John Hunt kept a daily diary of the expedition. He noted that Hillary was "quite exceptionally strong, abounding in a restless energy".

A new team

Early in the morning of 26 April, Hillary and Norgay climbed together for the first time. Their task was to reach Camp IV, set up during the Swiss expedition. This was to be the team's Advance Base Camp. It would be stocked with all of the supplies needed to reach the top of the mountain.

Camp comforts

It was a warm day. Norgay and Hillary, roped together, waded through deep, slushy snow that had softened with the sun's rays. They were hot and thirsty. In spite of these hardships, the two men worked well together. The two climbers found an unexpected treat waiting for them at Camp IV. The Swiss had left behind all sorts of supplies, including delicious cheese.

Near disaster

Hillary and Norgay decided to return to Base Camp. The two climbers stopped briefly at Camp II, where Hillary boasted that he could reach Base Camp within the hour.

All went well until Hillary decided to leap across a crevasse. He just reached the other side, but the edge of the crevasse broke off. Suddenly he was slipping downwards. His fate was in the hands of his partner.

The team's cook Thondup (crouching) prepared most of the food, here watched by Norgay and another Sherpa. A favourite treat was tinned peaches.

Fortunately, Norgay was a brilliant climber. He quickly grabbed hold of the rope and used all of his skill, strength, and experience to help Hillary climb up the side of the crevasse.

Safe and sound

The two men returned safely to Base Camp. The bond between them had been strengthened by this narrow escape. Hillary wrote to his parents that he and Norgay had become the "Tigers" of the expedition that day. They had shown the strength, courage, and fearlessness that they hoped would take them to the top of Everest.

Fully loaded, roped-together Sherpas cross a crevasse above Camp II. Crevasses were one of the expedition's greatest hazards.

The Tiger Medal

*Many of the Sherpas volunteered to join the lead climbers or to carry heavy packs through dangerous narrow tracks or **passes**. The highest honour for a Sherpa was to be singled out by the **Himalayan Club**. The club awarded the Tiger Medal to those who carried loads to the very highest points on the mountains. Norgay had been awarded the medal in 1938.*

Grateful thanks

After Norgay had saved Hillary from the crevasse, Hillary wrote in his diary:

"Without Tenzing I would have been finished today."

Aiming high

The weather worsened in the days after setting up Advance Base Camp, and the main climbing group were told to rest. Support teams slowly moved supplies up the mountain from Base Camp. Heavy snow meant that the Sherpas and other carriers constantly had to re-make their tracks in fresh snow. It was grim, hard work.

Onwards and upwards

Always restless and energetic, Hillary put himself forward for a climb to test the breathing equipment needed at the top of the mountain. This would again show his fitness, and that of Norgay. Hillary asked John Hunt if the pair could use oxygen sets in a fast climb from Base Camp to Advance Base Camp. Hillary believed that if they used the equipment successfully, the climb could be done in four hours instead of the usual nine.

Hunt agreed, and Hillary and Norgay set off at 6:30 a.m. on 2 May. It was clear and cold, perfect conditions for their mission. They quickly got used to the heavy equipment, and reached Advance Base Camp by late morning.

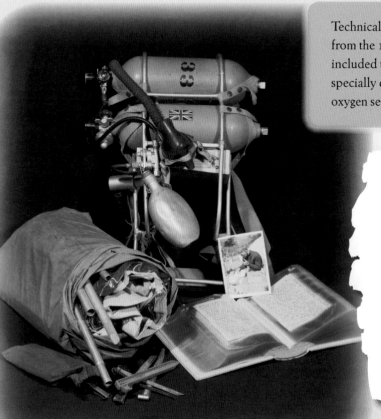

Technical equipment from the 1953 expedition included tent packs and specially designed oxygen sets.

Oxygen sets

*Previous attempts to reach the top of Everest had failed as climbers became exhausted with their slow progress. Two types of breathing equipment, or oxygen sets, were used on the 1953 expedition. These helped the **mountaineers** to overcome the lack of oxygen and climb higher and faster.*

Test of courage

Hillary and Norgay began their descent back to Camp II and then Base Camp, but the weather suddenly worsened. By the time they left Camp II, they were in a heavy snowstorm, or blizzard.

Tired and in near darkness, they bumped into ice walls and slid down snow slopes. Could they be completely lost? Hillary and Norgay needed to draw on all of their climbing experience to stay calm and find their way back safely. It was pitch dark when the pair finally saw the welcoming lights, comforts, and safety of Base Camp.

Hillary listens in as George Lowe talks on one of the expedition's radios. Short-range radio sets were used to communicate between camps and relay information such as weather reports.

Hazards and Dangers

In the first two weeks of May, a team of specially chosen climbers began to push onwards, above Advance **Base Camp**. They were at the foot of the huge Lhotse Face, a steep slope of snow and ice stretching above them for more than 1,000 metres (3,280 feet). They were in danger from **avalanches**, which are huge slides of snow or rock down a mountainside. Avalanches can roar downwards for many kilometres, carrying snow, ice, and rock, and sweeping away everything in their path.

The rumble of an avalanche releases built-up snow and ice, which cascades down the mountain.

Seasons on Everest

Attempts to climb Everest must be timed carefully. Before March, the winter weather is too cold and windy, with thick snow even on the lower slopes. But setting out too late might mean facing the warmer weather of the **monsoon** *season, usually from the end of May. Warm moist air blows up the mountain and cools, and its moisture falls as heavy snow. This can slide down the mountain in great avalanches.*

Tackling the Lhotse Face

On 11 May two climbers, George Lowe and **Sherpa** Ang Nyima, began the superhuman task of cutting **ice steps** and fixing ropes up the steep Lhotse Face. Sometimes waist-deep in snow, the two climbers pushed on as swirling blizzards made it hard to see more than a few metres. They were exhausted and felt frozen to the bone. The howling wind threatened to blow them off the face. It also made them feel even colder through the effect known as **windchill**.

Eventually, Lowe and Nyima hacked a route to the top. The whole expedition team was grateful to them for clearing a path. Now the other climbers could follow with tents, sleeping bags, and supplies such as food and fuel for the stoves.

Warm sleeping bags had been specially ordered by Hillary. They were filled with two layers of goose feathers which trapped air warmed by the climber's body. Inflatable air mattresses provided extra comfort.

A bleak place

By late May, the lead climbers had scaled the Lhotse Face to the South **Col**, where they set up Camp VIII at the higher end. A col is a flat area in a series of mountains. The South Col, at 7,894 metres (26,000 feet), is one of the nastiest places on Everest. With no place to shelter, it is cold and bare with ferocious winds.

To the limit

The howling winds on the empty, exposed South Col tested the climbers to the limit. **Altitude sickness** was a problem. The thin air at high altitude made even the simplest activities hard, and caused sickness and headaches. It took nearly an hour to put up two tents. Two of the team collapsed and lay face-down without moving for some minutes, but gradually recovered.

Camp VIII

John Hunt said of Camp VIII:

"As desolate a place as I ever expect to see."

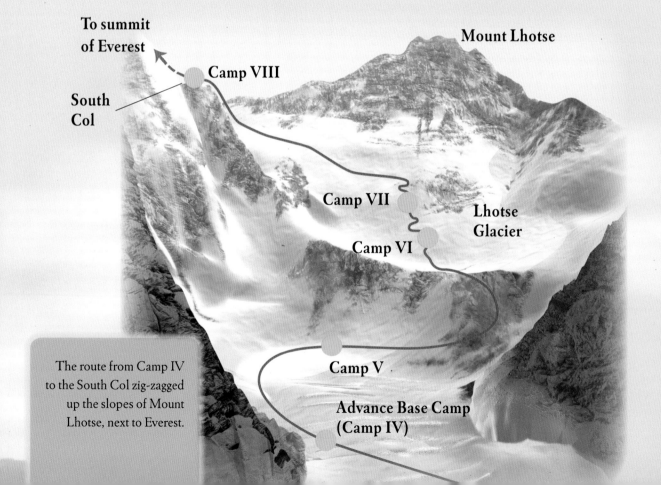

To summit of Everest

Camp VIII

South Col

Mount Lhotse

Camp VII

Lhotse Glacier

Camp VI

Camp V

Advance Base Camp (Camp IV)

The route from Camp IV to the South Col zig-zagged up the slopes of Mount Lhotse, next to Everest.

Showing the way

The expedition hit a new problem. Many of the Sherpas who had carried heavy loads up to Camp VII at the foot of the Lhotse Face were completely exhausted. Tenzing Norgay proved his ability as a Sherpa leader or **sirdar**. He encouraged them to continue, and on 22 May, he led the team of carriers up the Lhotse to Camp VIII.

On the night of 25 May, five climbers lay in their tents at Camp VIII, fully clothed in their sleeping bags. It was one of the most miserable nights of the journey, but as Hunt said: "The assault is on." The expedition was ready to try for the **summit**!

Tents for the high camps

The two-person pyramid-shaped tents used for the higher camps had been thoroughly tested before the expedition. High-tech materials made them exceptionally strong and wind-resistant. On the South Col, the climbers crammed into each of these tents, "packed in like sardines".

This photograph shows the two-man pyramid tents at Camp VIII on the windswept South Col.

Push to the Summit

Towards the end of May, the expedition was going to plan and the weather improved. John Hunt decided on two attempts to reach the top. The **summiteers** would need basic supplies and tents to be carried from the wide-open South **Col** to a final camp, as high as possible. They would not have the strength to carry these supplies themselves and then get to the top.

The first assault

Early on the morning of 26 May, Hunt and **Sherpa** Da Namgyal set off from Camp VIII with packs containing a tent, food, oxygen, and fuel. The two climbers selected for the first assault were Tom Bourdillon and Charles Evans. When Hunt and Da Namgyal could climb no further, they left their loads. Bourdillon and Evans continued past them, going higher than anyone had been before.

Yetis

Places like the South Col could be good for spotting the yeti. The Sherpas believed in this huge, human-like hairy animal, and early Himalayan explorers reported strange, large footprints in the snow.

Hillary showed an artist's impression of the yeti to news reporters before his 1960 expedition, but failed to find proof of the beast.

Iced up

Bourdillon and Evans started well, but slowed down as their oxygen tanks started to freeze. Conditions worsened and the oxygen ran low. Could they climb the final few hundred metres? It was an agonizing decision. The risks of low oxygen supplies and faulty equipment were too great. They reached the slightly lower South **Summit**, at 8,750 metres (28,707 feet), but did not get to the true summit.

So near...

Reluctantly, the two climbers began the slow descent to the South Col. At times they slipped, slid, and almost fell. They arrived at Camp VIII, their faces covered with frost, looking "like strangers from another planet".

Bitter disappointment

Bourdillon was very frustrated by not reaching the top. Also the oxygen apparatus he and Evans were using had been designed by himself, with the help of his father. It was a double disappointment.

Here Tom Bourdillon rests on the first summit attempt of 26 May. He and Evans did not quite make it to the top.

The last camp

On the morning of 28 May, five climbers set off from the South Col for the second assault on the summit. Three took the lead, cutting steps for Edmund Hillary and Tenzing Norgay to follow. This would help Hillary and Norgay to save energy for their final push on to the top. Nevertheless, all five climbers groaned under the weight of their heavy packs.

Heave!

After climbing for about 450 metres (1,470 feet), they reached the supplies that Hunt had dumped, which included a special lightweight tent. This would be set up as Camp IX, the highest camp. Hillary loaded this tent on to his already heavy backpack. He was now carrying many more times the amount thought possible at this **altitude**.

A safe place?

The five climbers spent some time searching for a spot safe enough to pitch the tent. It was nearly time for the three lead climbers to head back down, before their oxygen ran out. Finally, they found a narrow, sloping ledge just big enough for the tent. After good luck wishes, the three headed back to the South Col, leaving Hillary and Norgay. The two men began to prepare for a night in the final camp, at more than 8,500 metres (27,900 feet).

Highest Camp

For their last camp, Hillary and Norgay managed to clear snow, ice, and rubble from two patches, each just large enough to lie on. One patch was slightly higher than the other, with the tent across the 'step'. Just beyond, the ledge sloped sharply downwards. **Tent pegs** *were useless in the soft snow. Instead,* **support ropes** *were weighed down by oxygen tanks buried in the snow. It was far from safe!*

Dropping off to sleep

Edmund Hillary said of Camp IX:

"Tenzing seemed quite unaffected by the fact that the edge of the tent overhung the south face of the mountain."

Hillary and Norgay set off from the South Col to Camp IX, their last stop before the summit.

A long, cold night

Hillary and Norgay were now below Everest's South Summit, huddled in the tiny Camp IX tent, pitched on an uneven ice ledge. They faced a very cold night. To cut down their loads, they had left the outer layer of their sleeping bags at the South Col. They prepared a simple meal on their small stove.

The North Face of Mount Everest glows in the rising sun.

The final meal

Hillary and Norgay's last meal at Camp IX:
- *Chicken noodle soup*
- *Sardines on biscuits*
- *Dates and apricots*
- *Honey and jam*
- *Hot lemonade.*

Into the night

The space in the tent was so limited that Hillary, a tall man, could not sleep at full stretch. He also decided that they would have to limit the oxygen that they used to help them sleep. At 9:00 p.m. they dimmed the light. Outside, the wind howled, tugging at the buried ropes that held the tent above an almost sheer drop of hundreds of metres.

The hours pass

At 11:00 p.m. the two men were awoken by the wind and cold. They passed the time until 1:00 a.m. by making hot lemon drinks. After another two hours of broken sleep, they woke again. The temperature was well below freezing, and they shivered in their sleeping bags for another hour.

The day starts early high up in the mountains. At 4:00 a.m. the two climbers emerged from the tent to a clear, cold day, perfect conditions for climbing.

Boots on or off?

On their night at Camp IX, the two climbers slept fully clothed. Norgay kept on his boots for extra warmth. Hillary took off his so that he could put on dry socks. But he woke to find his boots were frozen solid. When the climbers fired up the stove, Hillary used it to thaw his frozen footwear.

The final climb

At 6:30 a.m. on 29 May 1953, Norgay and Hillary began the final journey to the summit. There were still many hazards before them. At times during that morning, they were knee-deep in loose snow. While climbing a steep slope, the surface snow shifted, carrying Hillary with it. He fell a metre (three feet) before coming to a halt, while the snow disappeared into the distance below.

The final obstacle

As well as picking out a safe route to the summit, Hillary had to constantly check the oxygen supply. The climbers needed enough to get to the top and safely down again. With their oxygen running low, the two men came to a rock face. It was too slippery to try and climb hard rock in the **crampons** fitted to their boots for ice climbing. There had to be another way. The next few minutes would be some of the most nerve-jangling of the whole expedition.

Hold on tight!

Hillary saw a **cornice**, an overhanging mass of snow and ice, attached to the rock. The cornice had started to come away from the rock, leaving a crack stretching upwards between the rock and ice. As Norgay stood below, Hillary crawled into the crack. Grasping the rock in front of him, he pulled himself further in. He jammed his crampons into the ice.

Leaning back to lever against his oxygen cylinder, Hillary forced his way up the rock at his front. Too much pressure and the whole cornice might break off. Also, as he climbed, the safety rope that held him to Norgay below began to tighten. But it was just long enough. Hillary pulled himself through the crack at the top of the cornice, paused for breath, and signalled Norgay to follow. Surely they were now near to the top?

Walking the "knife-edge"
Hillary described the narrow ridge to the main summit as a knife-edge covered with snow and ice. The two men inched slowly along, knowing that a piece of overhanging ice might break off at any moment, and send them crashing downwards.

Nerve-wracking
Edmund Hillary wrote of his cornice climb:

"My nerves were taut with suspense."

Hillary and Norgay roped together for their attempt on the summit.

The Top and Back

Hillary and Norgay continued along the ridge, hoping the **summit** would come into view. But the ridge seemed to go on and on. They were now very tired and still cutting **ice steps** into the sloping ridge. Just as Hillary doubted if they could keep going, he looked up and saw a snowy peak that dropped away on all sides. In his own words: "A few more whacks of the **ice axe**, a few more weary steps, and we were on the summit." It was time to celebrate, take photographs, and appreciate the widest view in the world.

The dream comes true

Talking about reaching the summit, Norgay said:

"We stepped up. We were there. The dream had come true."

Hillary wrote:

"We shook hands ... and thumped each other on the back."

Edmund Hillary took several pictures from the "top of the world". This one looks out to the west.

The descent

The two climbers journeyed back down with great care. They reached Camp IX at about 2:00 p.m. and then made it to the deserted South **Col** camp for the night. Next day, they were joyfully reunited with the rest of the team at Advance **Base Camp** (Camp IV). Everyone hurried into one of the large tents for food and hot drinks, and to hear the thrilling story of the final ascent.

One climber recalls Hillary saying: "Wouldn't Mallory be pleased if he knew about this." During their 15 minutes on the summit, Hillary and Norgay had looked briefly for signs of Mallory and Irvine, the climbers who disappeared in 1924. They found nothing.

Hillary said that "high-**altitude** tea" did not have the best flavour. Here, as he and Norgay sip their first cups back at Camp IV, it must have tasted good.

Telling the world

The expedition team had been on Everest for seven weeks. During this time a young newspaper reporter, James Morris, stayed at Base Camp and reported on events for the British newspaper *The Times*. There was huge interest in all parts of the world. Morris wanted to be sure that if the team succeeded, his newspaper was first with the story.

Slow mail

It was difficult to send news from Base Camp. There were radio receivers but no **transmitter** or telephone. Morris had to find a way of getting his written reports back to London. The quickest way was to pay a young **Sherpa** "runner" to carry the story to Kathmandu, a 240-kilometre (150-mile) journey that took at least six days. From there, it could be sent by radio to the Indian **Embassy**, then to London.

During April and May, the runners took updates to Kathmandu. Morris was worried about other reporters waiting in the area. They also wanted to be the first with the big story.

The secret code

Reporter James Morris was first with the Everest news because he discovered a radio transmitter in a village only two days' walk from Base Camp. He could only use this once, or other reporters might discover it. Also, to make sure the news got to London in secret, he decided to send the message in code.

Hillary used a 1935 Kodak Retina camera to take the first-ever photographs from the summit of Everest.

Breaking the news

On 30 May, a few hours after Hillary and Norgay told their story to the team at Camp IV, Morris had sent a message to the radio station he had found nearby. The coded message was radioed in stages to London. On 2 June, Morris turned on the radio at Base Camp to hear the news. The story had first appeared in *The Times*.

On 2 June 1953 Britain had a double cause for celebration. The British team had reached the top of Everest and a new queen, Elizabeth II, was crowned. This picture shows a page from *The Times* newspaper on that day.

Communications

In the early 1950s, most people kept up to date with news by listening to the radio or reading newspapers. However, this was changing. On 2 June 1953, the same day the Everest news broke, Elizabeth II was crowned Queen of England. Millions of people around the world watched the event live on a new form of communication – television.

Reasons for Success

As the celebrations died down, expedition leader John Hunt explained why the 1953 attempt on Everest succeeded when so many others had failed. Knowledge of Everest and careful planning were crucial. So was the very latest mountaineering equipment. Everyone understood that to succeed, the 1953 team needed to be exceptionally skilled and brave explorers. They cooperated as a team, and the expert climbers worked alongside an outstanding group of skilled **Sherpas**.

Good luck

The 1953 explorers needed luck in the one area out of their control – the weather. After some heavy snow in April, they had good conditions during the vital time of the last two weeks in May.

The heroes

Edmund Hillary and Tenzing Norgay were given honours in all parts of the world to mark their achievement. Hillary continued to journey over land and sea. He led an expedition to the South Pole in 1957. Since then, he has worked to improve the lives of the Sherpa people, especially children. Norgay continued to lead climbs in the Himalayas, particularly with young people, and died in 1986.

In 2003, 50 years after his achievement, Edmund Hillary (third from left) joins officials and the Crown Prince and Princess of Nepal, for anniversary celebrations.

The challenges ahead

In 1993, John Hunt encouraged young people to hold on to the spirit of adventure that had driven Hillary and Norgay to the top. They should seek out challenges and "create their own Everest".

Edmund Hillary is more cautious about the lessons learned. He reminds us that the 1953 team were not driven by the desire for fame and fortune. He also tells us to be careful when seeking to overcome challenges. Carelessness has cost many climbers their lives in the mountains.

Modern travel and improved climbing equipment mean Everest becomes more accessible year by year. Piles of bottles and bags, litter, old ropes, and discarded equipment gather on the slopes, left behind by climbers.

Everest today

*Hundreds of people have now climbed Mount Everest, and more do so every year. During the climbing season, there can be as many as 10 groups on the **icefall** at any one time! Sadly **Base Camp** has been turned into an untidy rubbish dump.*

The Route to the Top

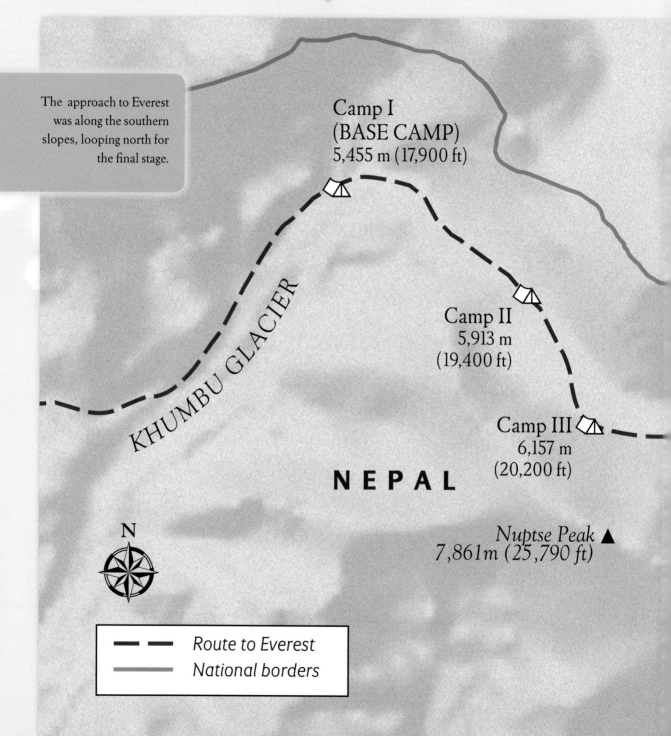

The approach to Everest was along the southern slopes, looping north for the final stage.

Camp I
(BASE CAMP)
5,455 m (17,900 ft)

Camp II
5,913 m
(19,400 ft)

Camp III
6,157 m
(20,200 ft)

KHUMBU GLACIER

NEPAL

Nuptse Peak ▲
7,861m (25,790 ft)

N

- – – Route to Everest
- —— National borders

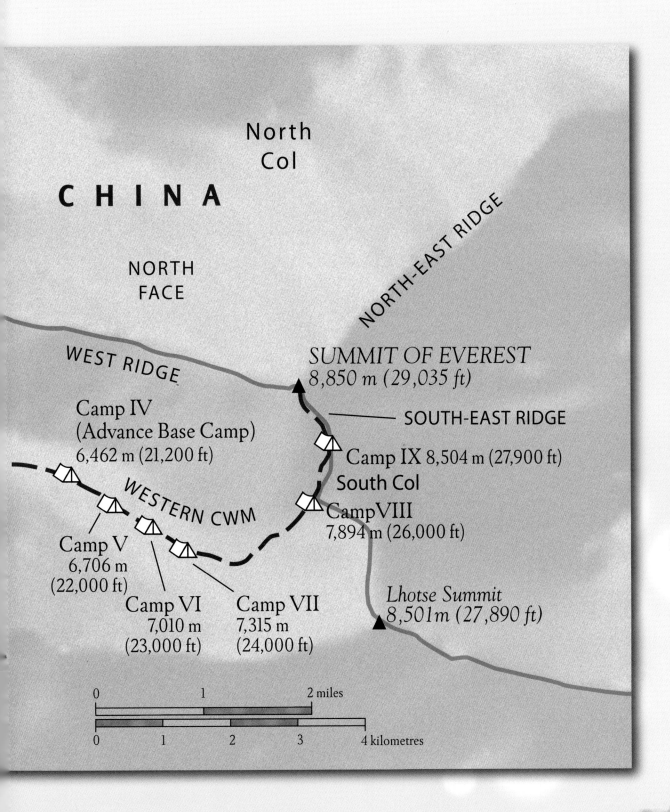

North
Col

CHINA

NORTH
FACE

NORTH-EAST RIDGE

WEST RIDGE

SUMMIT OF EVEREST
8,850 m (29,035 ft)

SOUTH-EAST RIDGE

Camp IV
(Advance Base Camp)
6,462 m (21,200 ft)

Camp IX 8,504 m (27,900 ft)

South Col

WESTERN CWM

Camp VIII
7,894 m (26,000 ft)

Camp V
6,706 m
(22,000 ft)

Camp VI
7,010 m
(23,000 ft)

Camp VII
7,315 m
(24,000 ft)

*Lhotse Summit
8,501m (27,890 ft)*

0   1   2 miles

0   1   2   3   4 kilometres

Timeline

1952	
5 November	Members of the expedition team are chosen
17 November	Members are measured for their clothing and equipment
1–10 December	The equipment is thoroughly tested
1953	
Early January	Supplies and transport are planned
Late January	Supplies are packed and boxed in the docklands of East London, UK
20 January	Climbers try their clothing and equipment for fit
12 February	Expedition members and supplies set out for India on the ship SS *Stratheden*
28 February	The ship arrives in Bombay (Mumbai), India
8 March	The expedition members and baggage reach Kathmandu, Nepal
10 March	The first walking group and 350 carriers leave Kathmandu
26–27 March	First Base Camp is established at Tengboche Monastery
29 March–17 April	The climbers rest and undertake fitness climbs as Base Camp is moved to the Lake Camp
13 April	Exploration begins of the Khumbu Icefall
15 April	Camp II is established
22 April	Camp III is set up at the top of Khumbu Icefall
24 April	Supplies are carried to Camp III
26 April–1 May	Supplies are ferried from Camp III to Advance Base Camp, Camp IV

3 May	Exploration climbs locate a site for Camp V
4 May	Advance climbers scale the Lhotse Face to Camp VI
5–8 May	Supplies are transported to Camp V
11 May	Lowe and Ang Nyima begin work on the Lhotse Face
18 May	Advance Base Camp is fully stored
21 May	A route is established through the final part of the Lhotse Face to the South Col
22 May	Supplies are taken to the South Col, Camp VIII
24 May	The first assault party reaches the South Col
26 May	The first assault is attempted. Bourdillon and Evans reach the South Summit but not the true summit.
27 May	The first assault party descends to Camp VII, but the second assault party is kept at South Col due to strong winds
28 May	The second assault party sets up Camp IX, the highest and last, for Hillary and Norgay
29 May	Hillary and Norgay climb from Camp IX to the summit and return to the South Col
30 May	The assault teams descend to Camp IV. Reporter Morris travels to Camp IV from Base Camp and returns with the story.
2 June	The teams assemble at Base Camp. News of success is broadcast on world radio.
20 June	The expedition returns to Kathmandu

Glossary

acclimatize allow the human body to get used to new conditions, such as lower oxygen levels at great heights. This avoids problems such as altitude sickness.

altitude height of a place or object, usually measured above sea level

altitude sickness tiredness, headaches, sickness, and light-headedness experienced in high mountains

avalanche large slide of snow (or rock) down a mountainside

Base Camp mountaineering camp set up as the starting point and main storage area for an expedition

Buddhism religion that follows the teachings of the Buddha, who lived in India in the early 5th century BC

col flat area or pass in a mountain range

cornice overhanging mass of snow and ice along a ridge, shaped by the wind like the crest of a wave

crampons metal frame with spikes fitted onto the bottom of boots, for climbing on hard snow or ice

crevasse large crack in a glacier, often very deep

cwm (pronounced coom) valley on the side of a mountain

embassy office of a country's representatives in another country

frostbite damage to the skin and body parts caused by extreme cold

glacier large, deep, long-lasting "river" of ice and hard snow

Himalayan Club club formed in 1928 to encourage and help travel and exploration in the Himalayas. Some of its members were Sherpas who worked on climbing expeditions.

ice axe special climbing tool used for cutting through hard snow and ice

ice steps stairs cut into hard snow or ice

icefall frozen cascade of ice

journal written account of a journey, like a diary

monastery place where a group of very religious people, usually monks or nuns, live and work

monsoon wind pattern that changes direction with the seasons. The Indian monsoon brings heavy rainfall.

mountaineer climber of high mountains

pass narrow mountain path

serac tower or pinnacle of ice

Sherpas name for the people of the Himalaya region. Also a term used for people who help on a journey, especially by carrying loads.

sirdar leader of a group of Sherpas on a mountain expedition

snow bridge layer of snow that sits across a crevasse

summit top point of a mountain

summiteer climber who has been selected to take part in the climb to the top

support ropes ropes or lines attached to a tent, also called "guys"

tent pegs large metal pins for support ropes that are buried or hammered into the earth or hard snow. They hold the lower ends of the ropes firmly in place.

terminal moraine pieces of rock and rubble deposited at the lower end of a glacier

transmitter piece of radio equipment that is used to send radio messages

windchill cooling effect of a strong wind when it takes away heat from the body

yeti unidentified creature that some people believe lives in the Himalayas

Further Information

Books

Hillary, Edmund. *High Adventure*
(Bloomsbury, 2003)
The 50th anniversary edition of the 1953 story told by one of the men who reached the top. This is a great tale of courage, skill, and endeavour, and has inspired many readers to undertake their own great journey.

Hunt, John. *The Ascent of Everest*
(Hodder & Stoughton, 2001)
The story of the 1953 journey told by the expedition leader John Hunt. His description of how he chose the climbers for the final assault is particularly gripping.

Jenkins, Steve. *The Top of the World: Climbing Mount Everest* (Houghton Mifflin, 2002)
Filled with facts about Everest, maps of the climbing routes, and stories about the daring mountaineers who have attempted to reach its summit.

Johnston, Alexa. *Sir Edmund Hillary, An Extraordinary Life* (Dorling Kindersley, 2005)
Packed with original photos, this book tells the story of the 1953 Everest expedition in detail, and also Hillary's thrilling expedition to the South Pole and return to the Himalayas.

Morris, Jan. *Coronation Everest*
(Faber and Faber, 2003)
The story of how the news about the Everest success was told to the world is almost as exciting as the journey itself.

Stephens, Rebecca. *Eyewitness Guides – Everest*
(Dorling Kindersley, 2001)
Plenty of facts and features about Everest and other mountain regions, descriptions of life in the mountains, famous journeys, and information on climbing equipment, techniques, and mountain rescue.

Websites

www.pbs.org/wgbh/nova/everest
A site with many exciting features and stunning photos. A section on climbing Mount Everest describes the effects on humans at high altitude.

http://teacher.scholastic.com/activities/hillary/
This site includes a detailed account of Hillary and Norgay's expedition, "Relive the Trek". There is a glossary of mountaineering terms, and an interview with Edmund Hillary about how he felt during the 1953 ascent.

http://magma.nationalgeographic.com/ngm/0305/feature1/
This site includes highlights from the *National Geographic* issue celebrating the 50th anniversary of the 1953 expedition. There are also 3-D maps, Everest wallpaper, and you can even send a postcard from the top of the mountain!

Places to Visit

Rheged Discovery Centre
Redhills, Penrith, Cumbria CA11 0DQ
Tel 01768 868000

Home of the permanent National Mountaineering Exhibition, the centre also regularly shows films on its giant screen, including a daily showing of *Everest*. This film tells the story of the mountain's discovery, its people, culture, and spirit, and how it was climbed, with digital surround sound and superb picture quality.

Sir Edmund Hillary: Everest and Beyond

A moveable exhibition celebrating Hillary's life, including the conquest of Everest. It has travelled to various venues including the Explorers Hall, National Geographic Society, Washington, DC, USA, and Auckland Museum, New Zealand, also Otago Museum, Dunedin, New Zealand.

Index